An Alien ASKS

Why do humans have two legs?

Philip Ardagh

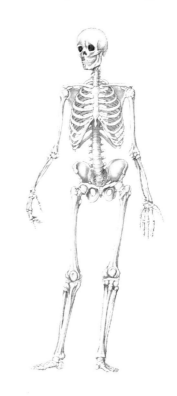

Belitha Press

First published in Great Britain in 1996 by
 Belitha Press Limited
London House, Great Eastern Wharf
Parkgate Road, London SW11 4NQ

Reprinted in 1997

Editor: Maria O'Neill
Designers: Guy Callaby and Helen James
Picture Researcher: Juliet Duff
Consultant: Steve Parker

ISBN 1 85561 540 1 (Hardback)
ISBN 1 85561 592 4 (Paperback)

Printed in Italy

British Library Cataloguing in Publication Data for this book is
available from the British Library.

Photographic credits:
All Sport/Tony Duffy: 6. Bubbles/L.J. Thurston: 28.
Scott Camazine:SPL: 7bl.
Collections/Anthea Sieveking: 24. Adam Hart Davis/SPL: 11c.
Chris Fairclough Colour Library: 12b, 13r, 18. Image Bank/G & M
David de Lossy: 16.
NASA/SPL: 14. Reflections/Jennie Woodcock: 20-1, 22.
J.C.Revy/SPL: 29. Rex Features: 25. Tony Stone Worldwide: 10
David Madison; 26-7. Zefa: 8.

Illustration credits:
Frank Kennard and Eugene Fleury: 6, 7, 11, 12, 15, 16, 17b, 19, 25.
Kevin Lyles: 8, 18, 23b, 27.
Simone End: 9, 17t, 20, 23l, 30.
Guy Callaby: 13, 24, 29.
Aliens by Graham Rosewarne

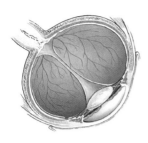

Contents

Meet the alien

You probably have a friend or someone in your family who is always asking questions, such as:

> Why does this happen?

> What makes it do that?

> How many are there?

In fact, that person might even be you. The one who is doing all the asking in this book isn't a person at all. It's an alien from outer space.

This particular alien likes asking questions about *everything*, but it won't answer many questions about itself.

We don't know whether the alien is a he or a she, or which planet it comes from. What we do know is its name . . . but it's very long and difficult to spell using any of Earth's languages. We also know that it is very friendly and interested in the planet Earth and what goes on here.

In this book, we answer the alien's questions about the human body – in other words – questions about *us*. The alien looked surprised when we told it that two-thirds of a human is made up of water, but it's true.

Perhaps the answers in this book will answer some of the questions you have about the human body. Some answers might set you off on your own investigations.

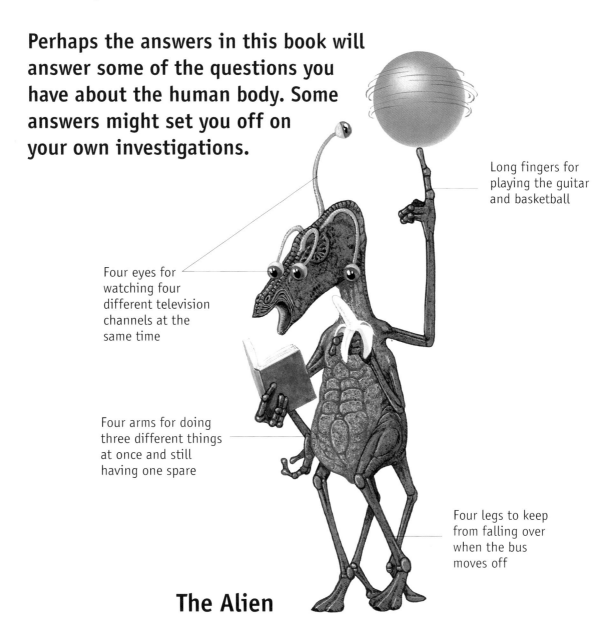

Long fingers for playing the guitar and basketball

Four eyes for watching four different television channels at the same time

Four arms for doing three different things at once and still having one spare

Four legs to keep from falling over when the bus moves off

The Alien

Some of the more difficult words in this book are printed in **bold** when they first appear. This shows that these words are explained in the glossary on page 31.

How is a human held together?

Humans are held together from the inside, by a group of bones called a skeleton. A skeleton is what gives us our human shape. We're also held together on the outside by a waterproof covering we call skin.

What does your skin do?

Our skin keeps out the rain. It keeps our insides on the inside (where they should be), and helps to control our body temperature. We also use our skin to feel the world around us.

▼ *Skin is made of two layers, the dermis and epidermis*

pain sensors
make us feel pain when something is hurting our skin

heat sensors
sense the temperature around us

touch sensors
let us feel how rough or smooth things are

sebaceous glands

pressure sensors
help us feel how hard our skin is being pushed

sweat gland produces water which leaves our bodies as drops of sweat and helps us cool down

epidermis

dermis

What are bones like?

Bones are hard on the outside and slightly spongy on the inside. They have jelly-like **marrow** in the middle.

◄ *This diver is about to splash into the water. The water will not soak through his skin into his body because his skin contains sebaceous glands. These cover him with a special waterproof oil.*

◄ *The skin section shown in this diagram is only 2mm thick.*

ALIEN EYE-OPENERS

●

The smallest bone in our bodies is the stirrup. We have one in each ear. Our longest bone is the femur. We have two of those too, one in each thigh.

●

We are shedding our skin all the time. Most household dust is dead human skin.

●

Sweating helps to cool our bodies.

Do all Earth creatures have skeletons?

Many do. Some creatures, such as insects, have their skeletons on the outside. Others have shells. But some creatures, such as jellyfish, have no shells or skeletons.

How many bones are there in a human skeleton?

It depends. Babies are born with about 350 bones. Most adults have 206.

What happens to a baby's extra bones?

Smart question, alien. They join together to form larger, fully-grown bones. Most (but not all) adults have the same number of bones in their hands or feet.

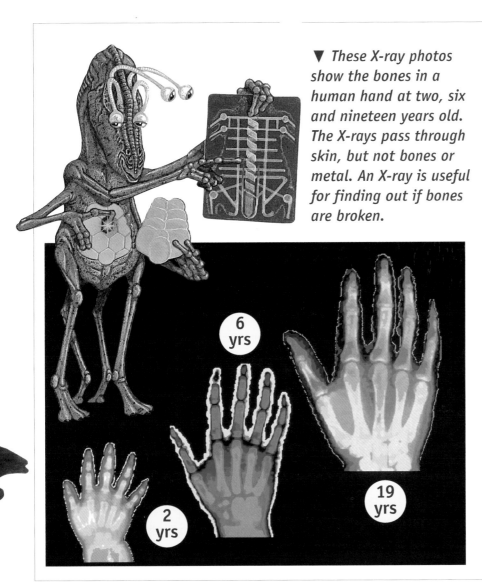

▼ *These X-ray photos show the bones in a human hand at two, six and nineteen years old. The X-rays pass through skin, but not bones or metal. An X-ray is useful for finding out if bones are broken.*

6 yrs

19 yrs

2 yrs

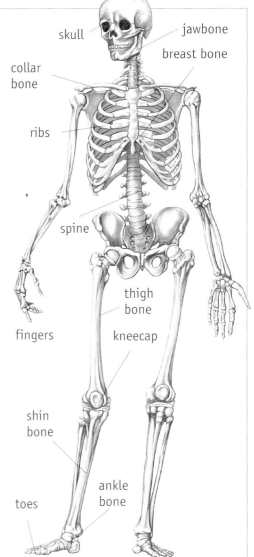

skull

jawbone

breast bone

collar bone

ribs

spine

thigh bone

fingers

kneecap

shin bone

ankle bone

toes

Why do humans have two legs?

Because one leg isn't enough, and three or more legs are unnecessary. If a person had just one leg, the foot at the bottom would have to be enormous. Our feet take the weight of our entire bodies.

But why don't humans need four legs?

Because our bodies are designed for walking upright. We don't have the speed of four-legged creatures, such as cats, but we have other advantages.

ALIEN EYE-OPENERS

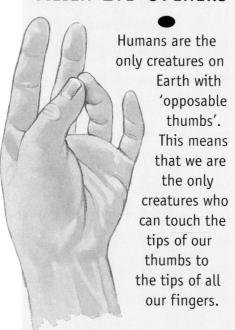

Humans are the only creatures on Earth with 'opposable thumbs'. This means that we are the only creatures who can touch the tips of our thumbs to the tips of all our fingers.

What advantages?

By having two arms instead of two front legs, our hands are free to do other important things, such as writing and making things. We can reach high, bend low and lead very different lives from our four-legged friends.

▶ *This girl's hands are free to hold an umbrella – she couldn't do this if humans walked on all fours.*

8

What are muscles?

Muscles are strong, pulling, body parts, usually fixed to our bones by **tendons**. A message is sent from the brain to a muscle to tell it whether to get shorter, or to relax and become longer. If a certain muscle shortens in one of our legs, for example, the knee bends. There are muscles all over our bodies.

How many muscles do you have?

Most people have about 640. That may sound a lot, but it takes about 30 muscles just to smile.

Which are the biggest, strongest muscles?

The biggest muscles in a human are the gluteus maximus muscles in our buttocks and thighs. The muscles that can apply the most pressure are our masseters – on either side of our mouths – letting us bite into things with incredible force.

MUSCLES IN THE HUMAN KNEE

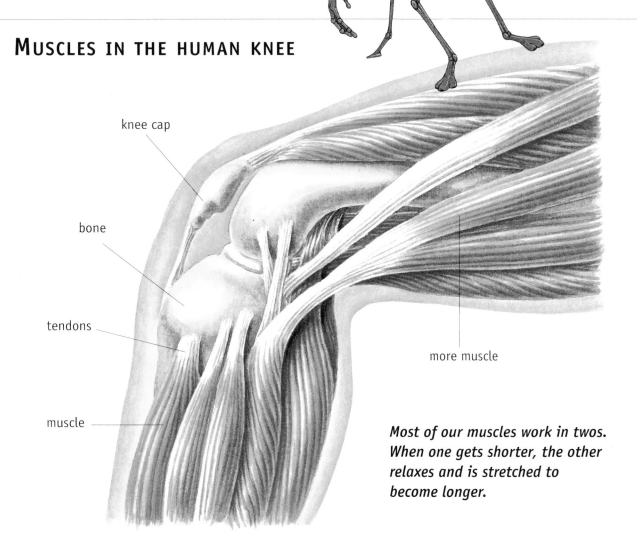

knee cap

bone

tendons

muscle

more muscle

Most of our muscles work in twos. When one gets shorter, the other relaxes and is stretched to become longer.

Why do humans have two eyes?

Because everything would look very flat if we only had one eye and it would be difficult to judge distances. Having two eyes solves this, so we don't need more than two.

But why are they in the front of your head?

To give us **binocular**, or **three dimensional (3-D)** vision. This means that both our eyes see the same object at the same time, but from very slightly different angles. Animals such as rabbits have eyes in the sides of their heads so they can see farther around them at once.

▼ *This tennis player's eyes view the tennis ball and her opponent the wrong way up. Her brain turns the images the right way up, and overlaps them to make a single 3-D image. She can then judge the position of the ball and her racket. Rabbits, with their eyes on the sides of their heads, can't do this . . .*

. . . Perhaps that's why you never see them playing tennis!

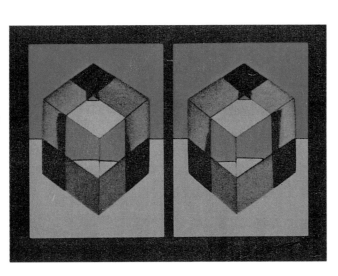

► *These two cubes are different views of the same cube. Put a piece of card on the line between them and bring your eyes close so each eye sees only one cube. You should now see a single 3-D cube.*

Why do humans cry?

If we get something in our eyes, our tear glands, which are under our eyelids, release water to try and wash it away. These drops of water are tears. Nobody knows why we cry when we are sad.

What are your eyelids for?

Eyelids act like curtains to keep out too much light, and like windscreen wipers to wipe away tears or dirt. We blink about 900 times an hour.

How do you see in colour?

We use special **cells** inside the backs of our eyes called cones. We have other cells called rods which are sensitive to light, but not colour.

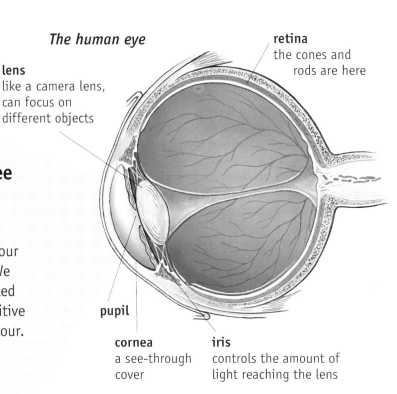

The human eye

lens
like a camera lens, can focus on different objects

retina
the cones and rods are here

pupil

cornea
a see-through cover

iris
controls the amount of light reaching the lens

◄ *Not everyone has the same number of cones in their eyes. Some people have fewer cones or cones that don't work properly so they see certain colours (usually reds and greens) in a different way. If you can see the number 57 among these dots, you see colours normally. If you see the number 35, it means you may have fewer cones. But don't worry, it's very common with humans.*

ALIEN EYE-OPENERS

●

Six muscles control the movement of each of our eyes.

●

The black dot in the middle of an eye, called a pupil, is really a hole. In dim light, the pupil gets bigger to let in more light.

●

A cat's eyes glow when light shines on them because there is a shiny layer called the tapetum at the back of its eyes. This reflects the light back out of the pupil.

What is a human's nose for?

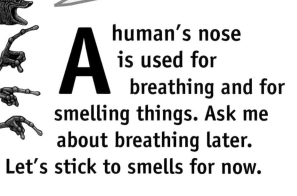

The nasal cavity

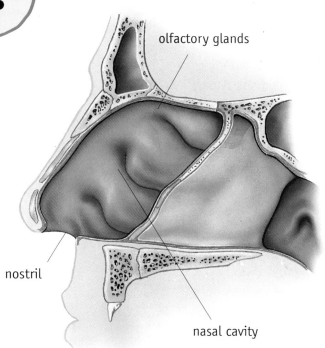

olfactory glands

nostril

nasal cavity

A human's nose is used for breathing and for smelling things. Ask me about breathing later. Let's stick to smells for now.

How do humans smell?

By not having a bath for a long time . . . That was a joke, alien. You mean 'how do humans smell smells?' don't you?

Yes. How do humans smell smells?

A smell is a chemical floating in the air. If we breathe in, some of the chemical is sucked up our nostrils. At the top of each nostril are tiny, sticky hairs (part of the olfactory glands) which detect smells. These hairs trap the smell and send signals to the brain, which identifies it.

▲ *Some scientists believe that a dog can probably sniff out 3000 million different smells.*

How many different smells can the human brain identify?

Many thousands. This sounds a lot, but a dog can probably smell many millions. Why not ask one later?

Why does sniffing make smells smell stronger?

Because more of the smell is sucked up the nostrils so more of the smell reaches the smell detectors and a stronger signal reaches the brain.

Why are some smells 'nice' and some smells 'nasty'?

You do ask difficult questions. It's probably because some smells are so strong that they leave a funny taste in our mouths and make our eyes water. These are the sort of smells we don't like.

So smell can affect taste?

Oh yes. A human's ear, nose and throat are all joined together. If we have a blocked up nose, and can't smell things properly, our food seems tasteless.

Can you prove this?

Yes. Ask some friends to wear blindfolds over their eyes and clothespegs over their noses. Give them each a peeled onion and tell them to take a bite. You'll be surprised how few of them are able to tell you what they are eating.

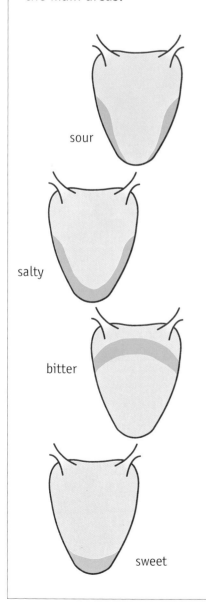

TASTE AREAS

Different parts of our tongues detect tastes more strongly. Here are the main areas:

sour

salty

bitter

sweet

▶ *This nose belongs to a boy who suffers from hayfever. At certain times of year, the air is full of pollen. The pollen irritates the inside of his nose. A sneeze will help to clear the pollen from his nose.*

A sneeze travels at just over 160 km/h... so it might be wise to turn the page, and find out about breathing.

Why do humans breathe?

▼ This astronaut is floating in space, but nowhere near the alien's planet. Unlike Earth, there is no air here, so there is no oxygen either.

Because if we didn't breathe, we would die, cease to function, be no more. You see, my alien chum, our bodies won't work without oxygen. The air around us is made up of about one-fifth oxygen. By breathing in air, our bodies can take in the oxygen we need.

But why do you breathe *out* air too?

Three reasons. First, to get rid of the rest of the air that isn't **oxygen**. Second, to breathe out **carbon dioxide**, a poisonous gas made by our bodies. Third, if we only breathed in but never breathed out, we'd soon burst.

When you've breathed in the air, where does it go?

Once air has come in through the nose and mouth, it goes down the windpipe and into the lungs. The oxygen passes from the air through the walls of our lungs into our blood.

◄ The astronaut is breathing oxygen from special tanks on the backpack of his suit. Without this oxygen supply, he would die.

What is blood?

A liquid which flows around the body carrying oxygen. Blood also carries carbon dioxide from the body into the lungs so that we can breathe it out. Blood is made up of red blood cells, white blood cells, platelets and **plasma**. The red blood cells contain **haemoglobin**, which carries oxygen and gives blood its red colour.

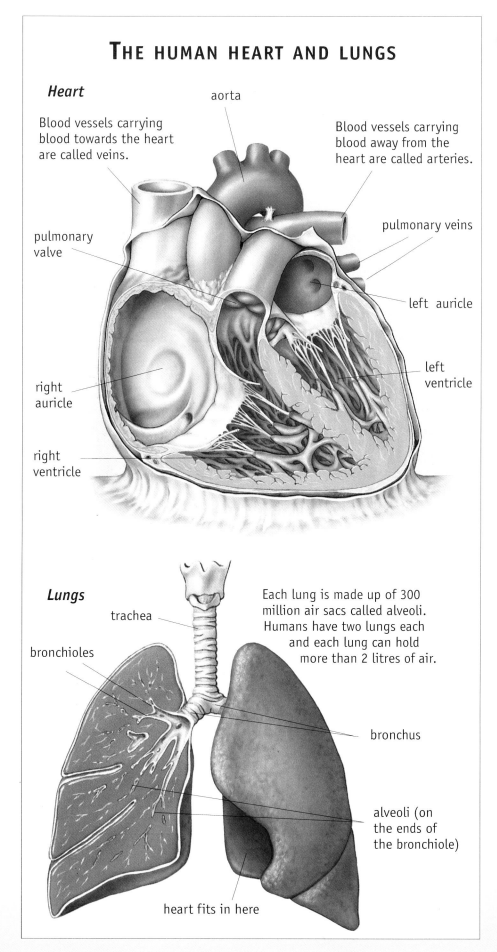

THE HUMAN HEART AND LUNGS

Heart

aorta

Blood vessels carrying blood towards the heart are called veins.

Blood vessels carrying blood away from the heart are called arteries.

pulmonary valve

pulmonary veins

left auricle

right auricle

left ventricle

right ventricle

Lungs

trachea

bronchioles

Each lung is made up of 300 million air sacs called alveoli. Humans have two lungs each and each lung can hold more than 2 litres of air.

bronchus

alveoli (on the ends of the bronchiole)

heart fits in here

What makes blood flow?

Each of us has a large pump inside us. This pump is called a heart. There are tubes, called blood vessels, that carry blood to and from the heart.

If blood is red, why are your veins blue?

Because haemoglobin in blood is only red when it is carrying oxygen. The blood in our veins has used up most of its oxygen. Once it has passed through the lungs to pick up oxygen, it will be bright red again.

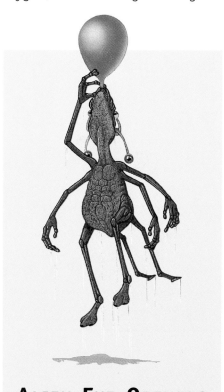

ALIEN EYE-OPENERS

●

Someone running very fast may need up to 70 litres of air a minute.

●

We can hear our heart pumping. That's what our heartbeat is.

Why do a human's ears stick out?

Most of a human's ear doesn't stick out at all. The main hearing part of the ear is *inside* the head. The part that sticks out, called the pinna, is designed to capture sounds, in much the same way that a satellite dish captures radio waves.

◀ *Some animals can swivel this part of the ear – the pinna – to capture sounds. Humans cannot do this.*

How does an ear 'capture' sounds?

A sound is a **vibration** from an object. When an object vibrates, it causes the air to vibrate around it. These vibrations are called sound waves. The waves hit the sticking-out part of the ear and bounce into the ear opening. The sound is now captured.

So what happens next?

The sound waves travel down a tube called the ear canal. At the bottom of the ear canal is an eardrum. The waves hit the eardrum and it vibrates like a tiny stretched piece of skin.

So humans hear noises if they are close to them?

Yes, but I haven't finished. Everything I've described so far happens in the outer ear. On the other side of the eardrum is the middle ear.

ALIEN EYE-OPENERS

●

Inside the inner ear are three semicircular canals. They help us to keep our balance.

●

Some animals can hear much higher notes than humans can. For example, a person cannot hear the sound that a dog whistle makes, but to a dog, it is loud and clear.

The ear of a human

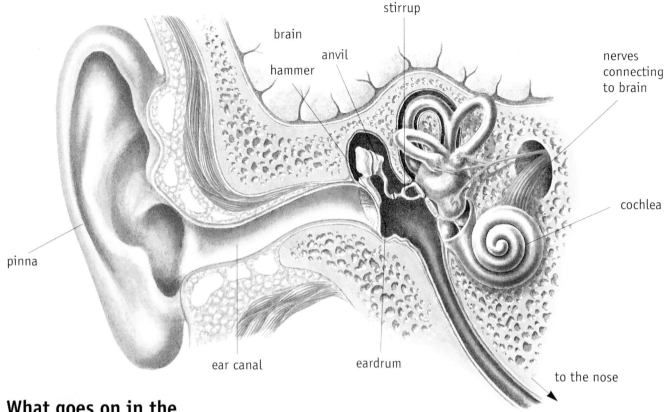

What goes on in the middle ear?

This is the bridge between the outer ear (with the eardrum) and the inner ear. The middle ear contains three tiny bones: the hammer, the anvil and the stirrup. These bones make the sound vibrations smaller but stronger before they reach the inner ear.

Does the sound's journey end in the inner ear?

Sort of. The cochlea, in the inner ear, is full of hundreds of 'hearing receivers' – hairs in a thin layer of jelly. The sound waves bend different hairs which send nerve signals to the brain to build up a pattern. From this pattern, the brain 'hears' a distinct sound.

So that's how you hear sounds, but how do humans make sounds?

At the top of the windpipe is our voice box. The **vocal cords** are inside it. They are pulled together to form a slit. Air goes through the slit and the vocal cords vibrate to make sound waves. Different sounds are made by changing the shape of the slit. We use our teeth, tongue and mouth to say words.

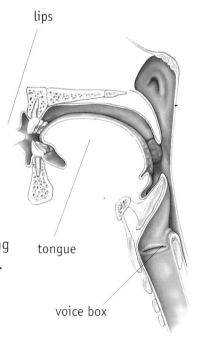

What goes on inside the human brain?

Much more than we know. Our brains control everything we do, everything we feel and everything we think. Even the experts don't know exactly how the brain does what it does, nor everything that it can do.

Where is the brain?

The brain is inside the head, at the top of the **spinal cord**. Nerves run from the brain down into the spinal cord. Other nerves run from the spinal cord to all parts of the body. The brain sends and receives messages to and from the whole body through the nervous system. The brain is protected by the skull.

◀ *This model shows a brain map of a body's sense of touch. The bigger the body part, the more sensitive it is – the brain gets more detailed messages from the skin in these areas. Some body parts are more sensitive than others – they feel more if touched or touching.*

◀ *This girl is deep in thought. She is trying to remember the music to a song. She is using a different part of the brain from the part she uses to remember a poster on her bedroom wall.*

What does it look like?

The main part of the brain – the cerebrum – looks like a giant walnut. It has two halves which are joined by a group of nerves called the corpus callosum.

Do the different halves do different things?

Yes. The left side of the brain controls the right side of the body, and the right side of the brain controls the left side of the body! The left side of the brain is involved with our creative skills – painting, drawing, singing. The right side is involved with logic and problem-solving.

THE HUMAN BRAIN

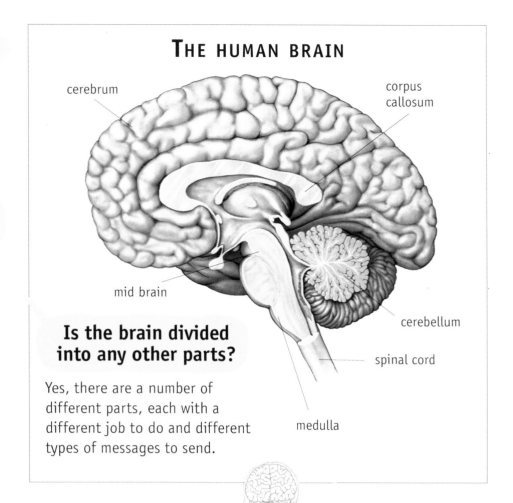

cerebrum

corpus callosum

mid brain

cerebellum

spinal cord

medulla

Is the brain divided into any other parts?

Yes, there are a number of different parts, each with a different job to do and different types of messages to send.

Are all memories the same kind?

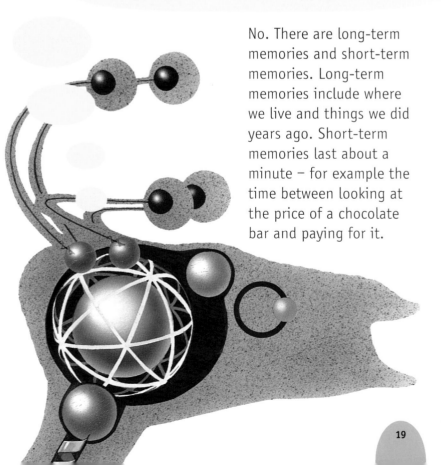

No. There are long-term memories and short-term memories. Long-term memories include where we live and things we did years ago. Short-term memories last about a minute – for example the time between looking at the price of a chocolate bar and paying for it.

How do the brain's messages get about?

Messages travel through the body's nervous system as nerve signals which are tiny electrical impulses. The **central nervous system** (the brain and spinal cord) deals with all the information sent from the rest of the body. These messages are sent along the correct routes in the brain by chemical 'switches'.

Why do humans eat?

Everything needs fuel to make it go. Cars need petrol. Plants need soil and sunlight. We need food to turn into fuel to keep us going. Going, in our case, means staying alive. We need to keep eating because we keep using up our fuel.

Where does food go once you've put it in your mouth?

On a journey that can last up to three days and nights. Along the way, different parts of the body add chemicals to the food. These help to break it down into tiny pieces that can be carried around in the blood. This is called digestion.

THE DIGESTIVE SYSTEM

Our teeth cut the food into small pieces as we chew and squash it. Watery saliva makes the food softer to swallow. The tongue pushes the food into our gullet. The gullet carries the food to our stomach.

The stomach blends the food until it is like a thick soup. This pulp goes to the small intestine.

In our small intestine, the nutrients are absorbed into the blood. The rest of the 'soup' goes into the large intestine. Here, some salts and water are absorbed into the blood. Waste carries on to the rectum.

What happens? If you follow the arrows on the diagram above, you'll soon see.

ALIEN EYE-OPENERS

●

Sweet things give us energy, but this energy doesn't last very long.

●

When we eat we swallow air with our food. Our bodies sometimes get rid of the air through our mouths. This is burping.

●

Kidneys make urine from chemicals and water that our bodies don't need. We have two kidneys.

▶ *This girl is hungry. She is eating an apple. This is only the beginning of the food's long journey through her body.*

What makes a human feel hungry?

Messages sent by the body to the brain. Sometimes, the smell or sight of food can make people feel like eating even if they're not hungry. It can make our mouths water. This is our saliva preparing to soften food that might be on the way.

Why do hungry humans' tummies rumble?

They don't always but, if they do, it's because air and digestive juices inside the stomach move around preparing for food!

Can you eat everything?

No, no, no! Our food must be made up of **nutrients** to be of any use to our bodies. Nutrients include proteins, carbohydrates, fats, minerals and vitamins. Each of these nutrients helps to keep our bodies healthy in different ways.

Which nutrient does what?

Good question, alien. Here's a chart to show you the answer.

Nutrient:	Use:	Found in:
Protein	body growth and repairs	meat, eggs, fish, cheese, nuts
Carbohydrates	energy	bread, pasta, vegetables, fruit
Fat	stored energy, warmth	milk, cheese, butter, meat, oil
Minerals	strong teeth and bones	fish, milk, cheese, vegetables

What about the vitamins?

Well spotted. Vitamins come from many foods and help the body in a variety of ways. There are over 20 types of vitamin. Here are just a few of them and some of the foods where they can be found.

Vitamin:	Use:	Found in:
A	helps eyesight	carrots, milk, eggs, butter
B	many things	meat, cereals, bread
C	health and repair	fresh fruit and veg
D	strong bones and teeth	fish, eggs, butter

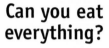

Is that all your bodies need?

No. We need to eat **fibre**. This is the part of food that is too tough to digest – but it is very important. It helps to carry the food through the body. We also need to drink water.

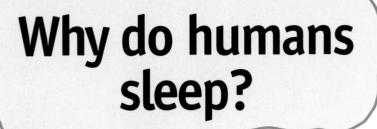

Why do humans sleep?

To give our bodies time to rest, relax, grow and repair themselves. Some scientists think that it gives our brains time to make sense of all the new information we have received during the day.

How does the body relax?

The eyes are closed. Breathing becomes slower. The heartbeat slows down, so blood is pumped around the body more slowly.

Why do humans sleep under covers?

Because our muscles are less active and our hearts beat more slowly so our bodies cool down. A duvet or blanket helps to keep us warm.

◄ *This girl is fast asleep. She is dreaming about an alien from outer space.*

How much sleep do humans need?

We spend about a third of our lives asleep!
The younger we are, the more sleep we need.
A baby can sleep for up to 20 hours a day.
A child of nine needs about 9 hours. Adults
don't need as much.

ALIEN EYE OPENERS

● We are taller in our sleep, because we are lying down! When we lie down, the discs in our spines are less squashed so we become longer.

● Some people talk in their sleep or even sleep walk. There are stories of sleep walkers carrying out simple tasks such as tying their shoelaces.

● When we're tired, we often yawn. This is because our lungs need to blow out stale air and take in fresh air.

What happens if you don't sleep?

If we don't sleep for a long time, our bodies stop working properly. Our brains get confused, our muscles get stiff and our eyelids droop. We don't properly react to anything.

What are dreams?

They are like films being played inside our heads. They are events made up by our brains – often a mixture of things which have happened and fantasies.

When do humans dream?

Every night, up to five times a night. We often forget when we've had a dream. When we dream, our eyes start to move about rapidly behind our closed eyelids. This is called Rapid Eye Movement or REM sleep. After a period of REM sleep, we go into much deeper sleep.

▼ *These pictures show some of the different positions a sleeping girl and her teddy bear take up in one night.*

Why do humans get bigger?

Because if we were born fully-grown, we wouldn't fit inside our mothers' tummies. Instead, we start small and grow.

ALIEN EYE-OPENERS

● There are more than 50 000 000 000 000 cells in each of our bodies. If you don't believe me, count them.

● About one fifth of a baby's weight is muscle. This changes as the baby grows up. An adult's muscles make up about two fifths of their total body weight.

● We lose over 18 000 hairs a year but (until we're old) new ones grow in their place.

Do human babies look like tiny adults, then?

Partly. But a baby is born with a brain that is very big compared to the rest of its body, so it needs a big head to store it. A baby's head is about a quarter of its height. Children aren't as hairy as adults either.

▲ *This baby looks a bit like an adult, but has a big head and less hair.*

▶ *This diagram shows the size of a boy's head in relation to the size of his body as he grows older. As a baby, his head is a quarter of his total height. As a fully-grown man, his head is only one eighth of his body size.*

24

When do humans get hairy?

When we reach **puberty**. That's when children grow body hair. Babies and children only grow thick hair on their heads. Girls reach puberty when they are between 10 and 12 years old. Boys reach puberty between 12 and 14 – their voices 'break' and become deeper. Puberty prepares the body for making babies.

But how do you grow?

Everything in our bodies is made up of cells. Cells grow and each one splits in two to make new cells. The more cells we have, the bigger we are. Our bodies make more and more cells until we are 18 to 20 years old. After that, our bodies only replace cells that have died. Chemical messengers called **hormones** help our bodies grow to adulthood.

Do all cells look the same?

No. There are lots of different kinds. Here's a picture of some of them.

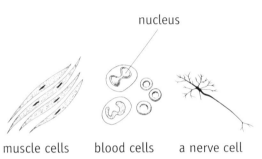

nucleus

muscle cells   blood cells   a nerve cell

▲ *These cells are enlarged so we can see them. Humans need microscopes to study cells. In the middle of each cell is the nucleus which controls what the cell does. When a cell splits, the nucleus does too.*

Is it true you can grow new teeth?

Yes. A baby's teeth start to appear when it is about five months old. Babies grow a set of 20 milk teeth. Between five and twelve years old, the milk teeth fall out and 32 adult teeth grow.

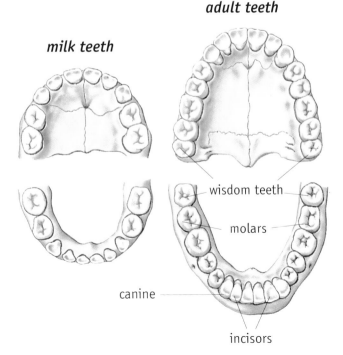

milk teeth

adult teeth

wisdom teeth

molars

canine

incisors

▲ *This man is fully grown and very tall. These children have lots more growing to do. Men are usually taller than women.*

Why do humans wrinkle with age?

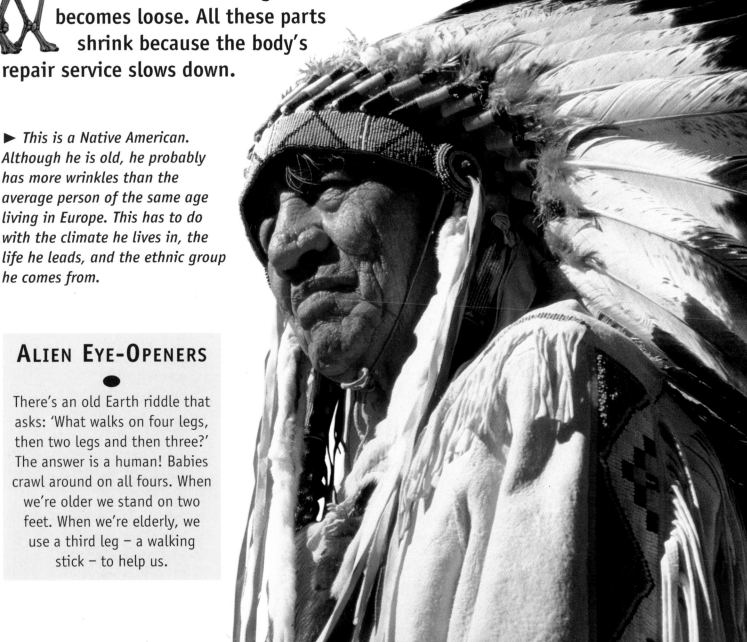

Because the older we get, the thinner and less stretchy our skin becomes. Not only that, our muscles and other parts begin to shrink, so the skin that's covering them becomes loose. All these parts shrink because the body's repair service slows down.

▶ *This is a Native American. Although he is old, he probably has more wrinkles than the average person of the same age living in Europe. This has to do with the climate he lives in, the life he leads, and the ethnic group he comes from.*

ALIEN EYE-OPENERS

●

There's an old Earth riddle that asks: 'What walks on four legs, then two legs and then three?' The answer is a human! Babies crawl around on all fours. When we're older we stand on two feet. When we're elderly, we use a third leg – a walking stick – to help us.

What does this repair service do?

It makes new cells all the time. For example, in a single human, two million blood cells die every second. But don't panic. The repair service replaces them with new ones.

When do humans start to age?

Most of us stop growing when we're about 20. After that, we begin to start ageing...but it's a very long process! It's not until we're about 55 to 60 that our body repairs slow down.

Why does a human's hair turn grey?

Human hair is made from a protein called keratin, which is greyish white. It gets its colour – blond, black, brown or red – from **melanin**. As we get older, there is less and less melanin in our hair, until there is only the colour of keratin left.

THE SIGNS OF AGEING

hair turns grey

eyesight not so good

hearing less precise

skin loosens

joints stiffen so a walking stick might help

What else happens to old people?

When we get old, our brains can take longer to work things out and our hearing gets worse. Our joints stiffen up, and we might even need walking sticks to support us when we walk around.

How long do humans live for?

In Europe and America, the average is about 75 years. Some of us live much longer though. There are records of people living to 120. (Women usually live a few years longer than men.)

Why don't all humans look the same?

A tricky one this, alien, because it depends what you mean. People of different ages, sexes, and ethnic groups can look very different from each other. People of the same age, sex and ethnic group can look very similar – until you look closely.

▼ *Although all three children in this family look different from each other, they all share a mixture of their father's and mother's genes. This makes them look similar in many ways.*

But why does a baby look like its father or mother?

The parts of human cells that decide what we look like are called **genes**. A baby's genes are a mixture of its father's genes and its mother's genes so the baby grows up to look like one or both of them.

So do brothers and sisters ever look exactly alike?

Yes, but only if they are identical twins. Our genes are found in our cells on tiny threads called chromosomes. These are made of a chemical called **DNA**. The only people who have the same DNA are identical twins because they share the same mixture of genes from both parents.

What do your genes decide?

What colour our eyes are, what colour our hair is, what colour our skin is, whether we are short or tall, the way we make certain gestures... this list goes on and on. Our final appearance is affected by our dominant genes.

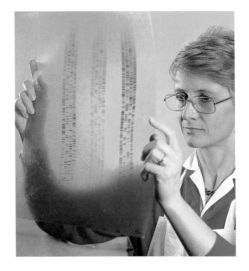

◀ *This scientist is looking at a DNA sequence taken from a living cell.*

GENES AND HEREDITY

What are dominant genes?

These are genes that cancel out the power of other genes. For example, the gene that gives a person brown eyes is stronger than the gene that makes eyes blue. If each parent has one brown eye gene and one blue eye gene, the baby is likely to have brown eyes because the brown eye genes are dominant.

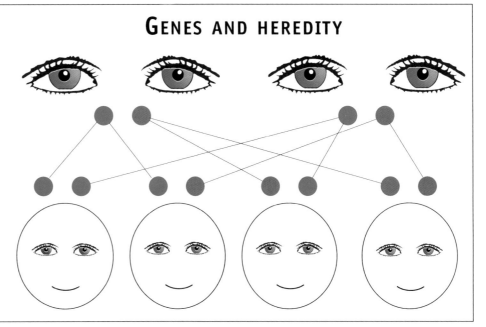

Why do people have different skin colours?

Over a very, very long time, our genes have helped us adapt to different weather in different parts of the world. Skin colour is one example of this. In hot, sunny places, people **evolved** dark skin to protect them from the sun's harmful rays.

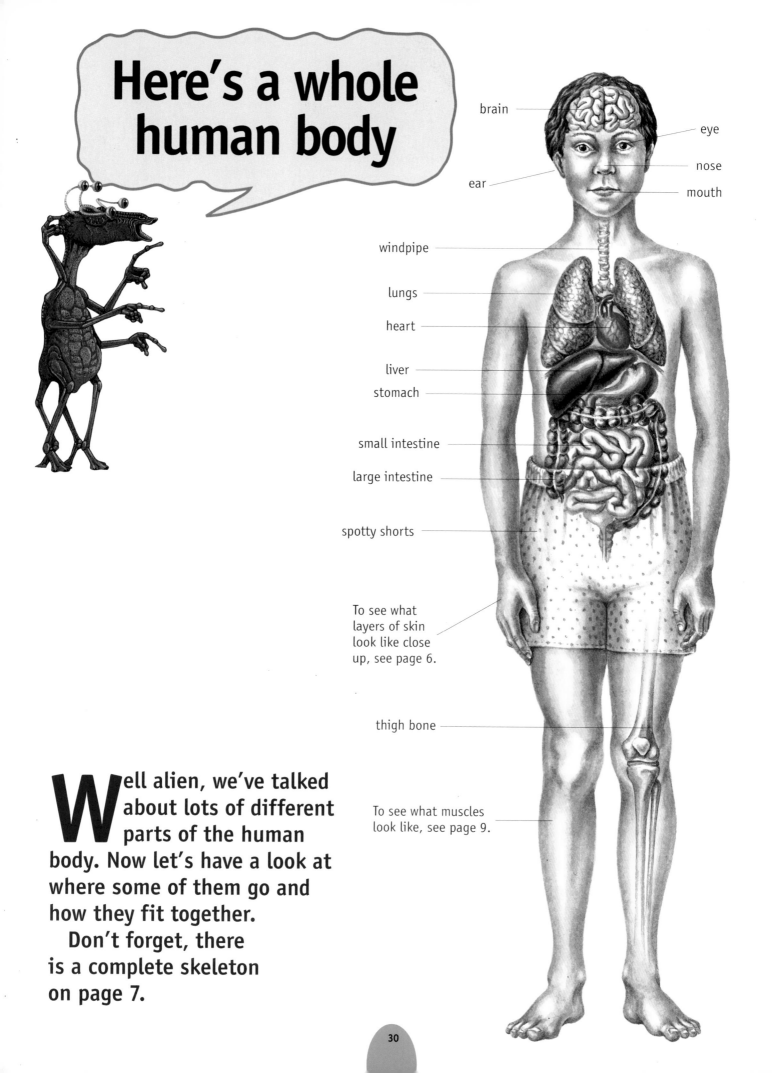

Here's a whole human body

brain

eye

nose

ear

mouth

windpipe

lungs

heart

liver

stomach

small intestine

large intestine

spotty shorts

To see what layers of skin look like close up, see page 6.

thigh bone

To see what muscles look like, see page 9.

Well alien, we've talked about lots of different parts of the human body. Now let's have a look at where some of them go and how they fit together.

Don't forget, there is a complete skeleton on page 7.

30

Glossary

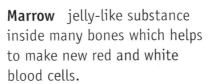

Binocular vision vision using two eyes which gives a three-dimensional (3-D) effect.

Carbon dioxide gas breathed out by people and animals and produced as a waste product by plants. It is found in the Earth's atmosphere.

Cells the basic part of a living thing, animal or plant.

Central nervous system the brain and spinal cord. The central nervous system controls all our actions.

DNA deoxyribonucleic acid. This is found in our genes and contains all the information needed to give living cells their characteristics.

Evolve gradually change characteristics (ie size, colour or shape) over generations.

Fibre food that passes through our bodies without being digested. It is needed for digestion to work.

Gene one part of a cell in all living things. Genes are passed from parents to children. They are what make us different from each other.

Haemoglobin substance in the blood that makes it bright red. It carries oxygen around the body.

Hormones chemical messengers which help our bodies to grow and to develop sexually.

Kidneys the parts of the body that remove unwanted waste from our blood and turn it into urine.

Marrow jelly-like substance inside many bones which helps to make new red and white blood cells.

Melanin coloured pigment which gives hair and skin their colour.

Nerves carry messages between the brain and other parts of our bodies. These nerve messages or signals help us to feel and move.

Nutrient any part of food that the body can take in and use. The body needs nutrients for things such as growth, repair and fighting infection.

Oxygen the colourless gas in air that humans need to breathe and stay alive.

Plasma clear, yellowish fluid which makes up part of the blood. The blood cells float in it.

Puberty when a child's body begins to turn into an adult's.

Spinal cord cord of nerves in the backbone joining the brain to the body's nerves.

Tendons thick, tough cords that join muscles to bones.

Three-dimensional vision (3-D) sight that creates the effect of depth and distance by showing a slightly different view of the same objects to each eye.

Vibration rapid shaking.

Vocal cords the part of the throat that can vibrate and make sound when air is passed through them. Vocal cords make it possible for us to speak.

Bye for now. I'll be back with more questions soon.

Index